THIS BOOK BELONGS TO...

Name: Age:

Favourite player:

2019/2020

My Predictions...   Actual...

The Seagulls' final position:

The Seagulls' top scorer:

Premier League winners:

Premier League top scorer:

FA Cup winners:

EFL Cup winners:

Contributors: Peter Rogers, Luke Nicoli, Paul Camillin & Ivan Butler

A TWOCAN PUBLICATION

©2019. Published by twocan under licence from Brighton & Hove Albion FC.

ISBN 978-1-911502-99-9

PICTURE CREDITS: Brighton and Hove Albion FC, Paul Hazlewood, Action Images and Press Association.

£9

CONTENTS

Mathew
RYAN

POSITION: Goalkeeper   **COUNTRY:** Australia   **DOB:** 08/04/1992

Goalkeeper Mathew Ryan joined the Seagulls back in the summer of 2017 ahead of the club's first season in the Premier League. Signed for a then club record fee from Valencia, Ryan has firmly established himself as Brighton's first-choice keeper. With excellent reflex saves, assured handling skill and a good command of his area, Ryan's presence gives great confidence to those playing in front of him.

SQUAD 2019//20

Gaëtan
BONG

03

POSITION: Defender   **COUNTRY:** Cameroon   **DOB:** 25/04/1988

Gaëtan Bong joined Albion in the summer of 2015 following a short spell with Wigan Athletic. The defender had previously made his name in France with Metz and Valenciennes before trying his luck in Greece with Olympiacos. A promotion winner with the Seagulls in 2016/17, Bong's club form has won him a return to the Cameroon international scene. The defender put pen to paper on a new Albion deal in May 2019, extending his stay on the south coast until June 2020.

Shane
DUFFY

04

POSITION: Defender   **COUNTRY:** Republic of Ireland   **DOB:** 01/01/1992

A key part of Albion's 2016/17 promotion-winning campaign, central defender Shane Duffy is a vastly experienced and well-respected member of the Seagulls' squad. Duffy currently boasts the mantle of being the club's most capped international. A reliable performer at the heart of the defence for both club and country, Duffy has become one of the first names on the team sheet for both Brighton & Hove Albion and the Republic of Ireland.

THE LEGEND JIMMY CASE

Following a successful spell with Liverpool, midfielder Jimmy Case joined the Seagulls in the summer of 1981 in a £350,000 deal. When his former club visited the Goldstone for a First Division clash in October 1981, Case took great delight at adding his name to the scoresheet in a thrilling 3-3 encounter.

Jimmy Case's goals proved pivotal in the Seagulls' never-to-be-forgotten run to the 1983 FA Cup Final. After Albion had dispatched Newcastle at the third-round stage, Case was on target in a 4-0 demolition of Manchester City in round four. Albion's reward for their victory over City was a fifth-round trip to Liverpool.

Always the man for the big occasion, Case relished taking on his former club in the FA Cup when Brighton travelled to Anfield in 1983. Despite the home side being strong favourites, the tie was evenly balanced at 1-1 when, with 20 minutes remaining, Case struck a stunning 25-yard drive past Bruce Grobbelaar to cause the upset of the round and take Albion to the quarter-final stage.

After his heroics in the FA Cup fifth round at Anfield, Case picked up from where he left off on Merseyside when Norwich City provided the Seagulls' quarter-final opposition at the Goldstone Ground. Case slammed home the only goal of the game after 66 minutes and was very much the toast of Sussex as Albion reached their first ever FA Cup semi-final.

On 16 April 1983 Jimmy Case opened the scoring in Albion's FA Cup semi-final meeting with Second Division Sheffield Wednesday at Highbury. Case unleashed yet another rocket-like shot to put Brighton in front and en route to a 2-1 victory that took the Seagulls to Wembley!

ANTHONY KNOCKAERT
v Crystal Palace (A)

2018/19

GOAL OF THE SEASON

As soon as the ball left his foot, it was always going to be a frontrunner for Albion's Goal of the Season, so step forward Anthony Knockaert for a stunning 74th-minute winner against Crystal Palace at Selhurst Park.

Picking the ball up on the right flank, the winger cut inside on to his left foot, took another touch, before unleashing a curling effort that flew into the top corner off a post – leaving Eagles keeper Vicente Guaita grasping at thin air.

It was a strike so spectacular that even when the Brighton fans erupted in the far corner of the Arthur Waite Stand, teammate Glenn Murray was left stunned on the spot, hands over his mouth, in disbelief!

"It's certainly the best I've scored for Brighton," recalls Anthony. "It was an unbelievable goal and I was really happy with it, especially as it handed us the three points, which is what we needed on the back of a win against Huddersfield the previous week.

"If you watch the video back, when I cut in I wanted to hit it first time but I didn't have enough space or a good enough angle to take it on, so I decided to give myself another touch. I then took the shot and it went perfectly. To be honest, from the angle I was shooting from I thought it was going to hit the crossbar, but when I saw it hit the post and then the back of the net, it was the perfect goal and a very important one as well."

RUNNER-UP

Florin Andone
v Crystal Palace (H)

A long clearance forward by Bernardo was met by the striker on the left flank, just inside the Palace half. He then outsprinted James Tomkins in a race into the box before cutting inside to drill the ball past keeper Wayne Hennessey.

It was the Romanian's second goal in a week having also scored against Huddersfield.

Lewis DUNK   05

POSITION: Defender   **COUNTRY:** England   **DOB:** 21/11/1991

Born in Brighton, central defender Lewis Dunk has progressed though the youth and reserve team ranks to become a regular face in the Albion defence in the Premier League era. Dunk has formed an extremely reliable central defensive partnership with Shane Duffy. After excelling at Premier League level, his club form has seen him gain international recognition with England and he won his first full cap against the USA in a friendly at Wembley in November 2018.

Dale STEPHENS   06

POSITION: Midfielder   **COUNTRY:** England   **DOB:** 12/06/1989

Now one of Albion's longest-serving members of the current squad, midfielder Dale Stephens joined the Seagulls back in January 2014 from Charlton Athletic. Stephens is now closing in on 200 appearances in a Brighton shirt and after helping the club secure promotion to the Premier League, he agreed a new long-term contract at the Amex. He scored his first Premier League goal in last season's 2-2 draw with West Ham United at the London Stadium.

Neal
MAUPAY
07

POSITION: Striker **COUNTRY:** France **DOB:** 14/08/1996

Striker Neal Maupay joined the Seagulls on the eve of the new 2019/20 season after agreeing a four-year deal with Graham Potter's side. Maupay shot to prominence with an impressive two-season scoring spell with Championship club Brentford. His 41 goals in 95 appearances for the Bees made him one of the most wanted players outside of the Premier League and he marked his Albion debut with a goal in the 3-0 opening-day win at Watford.

SQUAD
2019/20

 D Wears the Birmingham City captain's armband

 **Crystal Palace's nickname** **E**

A **Chelsea's Spanish skipper**

Danish head coach at Griffin Park **F**

B

Do you recognise this Championship club's crest

 **The Toffees play their home games here**  **G**

 H Longest serving Championship manager and a Millwall legend

 Scored the first home league goal of the season at the City Ground **C**

I Foxes' Nigeria international signing who wears No.8

J

Manchester City's Brazilian striker who was part of their 2019 Copa América-winning side

K

Polish international midfielder who was ever-present for Leeds United last season

L

This England international has been with the Red Devils since the age of 7

M

The Seagulls' Premier League top scorer last season

ANSWERS ON PAGE 62

15

AT THE TRAINING GROUND.....

Come three o'clock on a Saturday afternoon, the fans get to see their heroes in action at the American Express Community Stadium.

Matchday is the day the Seagulls' players, manager and coaching staff are all preparing for and focusing on throughout the week. All that preparation takes place at the club's training ground, well away from the watching eyes of the thousands of fans who flock to the Amex in hope of witnessing another winning performance.

The hard work begins in the summer months when the players all report back for pre-season training. The players are given a fitness programme to follow over the summer break and the first few days back at the training ground tend to involve a number of fitness tests. The results will enable Graham Potter's coaching and fitness staff to assess each player's condition and level of fitness to ensure they are given the right workload over pre-season, so that they are fully match fit and raring to go for the big kick-off.

A lot of the work done over the pre-season period is designed to help the players reach a level of fitness that they can maintain for the entire campaign and perform at their maximum throughout the season.

When it comes to winning football matches, it is well known that practice, dedication and preparation are all vital ingredients for success. However, in terms of strength and fitness, rest, recovery and diet also play crucial parts in a footballer's welfare. The Brighton players are not only given the best of surfaces to practice on, but also given expert advice and guidance to ensure that they are fully equipped for the Premier League challenges ahead.

Technology also plays its part in helping the Brighton stars perform to their maximum. Prior to taking to the training pitches, players are provided with a GPS tracking system and heart rate analysis monitors ensuring that all they do, can be measured, monitored and reviewed.

And if all goes to plan, the team's drive, commitment and meticulous preparation on the training ground during the week, will pay dividends on matchday.

THE LEGEND BOBBY ZAMORA

Having initially joined Albion on loan from Bristol Rovers in February 2000, Bobby Zamora marked his debut with a goal against Plymouth Argyle at Withdean Stadium on Saturday, 12 February. Zamora's strike against the Pilgrims was his first of six goals during that loan spell which helped trigger a permanent switch to the Seagulls.

While still on loan with Brighton, Zamora grabbed his first hat-trick for the club. A memorable treble came in what was only his third appearance in an Albion shirt as the Seagulls turned on the style to defeat relegation-bound Chester City 7-1 on 26 February. Zamora netted the first two goals of this seven-goal romp at Chester in the 18th and 21st minutes of the game. He ensured he would return home with the match ball when he completed his hat-trick from the penalty spot nine minutes into the second half.

Zamora's first full season with Brighton proved to be a great success as the popular striker netted an incredible 31 goals in all competitions for the Seagulls. His goal haul included two hat-tricks and five braces. He ended the 2000/01 campaign with a Third Division title-winners' medal as Albion landed top spot with a 10-point cushion.

The goals continued to come Zamora's way once again in 2001/02 as he and his Brighton teammates achieved an incredible back-to-back promotion triumph. Despite the step up in standard, Zamora went one better than the previous campaign by this time notching an amazing 32 goals in all competitions, including a run of scoring in ten consecutive appearances.

After leaving the Seagulls in 2003, Zamora played for Tottenham Hotspur, West Ham United, Fulham and Queens Park Rangers. In the summer of 2015, he made an emotional return to Brighton for the 2015/16 campaign. The returning hero scored the first goal of his second spell when he grabbed a dramatic 89th-minute winner away to Leeds United to secure a 2-1 win in October 2015.

Women's Team

The Seagulls are currently enjoying their second season of FA Women's Super League football and continue to go from strength to strength under former England coach Hope Powell.

The team took their inaugural top-flight season in their stride, finishing the campaign some 19 points clear of bottom-placed Yeovil Town.

In a league that consisted of the likes of Manchester City, Chelsea and Liverpool, the Seagulls competed well throughout the campaign, with the highlights being a 2-1 win against fourth-placed Birmingham and a home game against champions-elect Arsenal, played at the Amex in front of a WSL record crowd of 5,365.

Albion certainly grew in stature during the second half of the campaign and Powell believes it was the hard work put in on the training ground that started to pay dividends.

"The players got their heads around the demands after the Christmas break and really came back stronger," she recalls. "We drilled into the players that we must do the basics well, and pushed ourselves on. That message of striving to be better sunk in and a lot of the detail we try to put into the players, to make them one per cent better, allowed them to improve."

The 2019/20 season will again test the Seagulls, with FA Women's Championship winners Manchester United having entered the top flight for the first time, where they have been joined by runners-up Tottenham Hotspur.

"The league is tougher this season so our primary aim is to stay in the division and try to build on what we've achieved," Powell adds. "We want to consolidate our position but we have to recognise that this is the first time the players have been in a full-time professional environment.

"The players are more robust now compared to when I started, but this season we've had to demand more from them, and to bridge that gap with the top sides, we're going to have to demand even more."

Yves
BISSOUMA

08

POSITION: Midfielder   **COUNTRY:** Mali   **DOB:** 30/08/1996

Mali international midfielder Yves Bissouma joined the Seagulls from Lille in the summer of 2018. After two seasons in France, Bissouma agreed a five-year contract at the Amex and made his debut in the opening-day match away to Watford. The midfielder featured in 28 Premier League fixtures in 2018/19 and played a key role in the Seagulls' run to the FA Cup semi-final.

Leandro
TROSSARD

11

POSITION: Midfielder   **COUNTRY:** Belgium   **DOB:** 14/04/1991

Winger Leandro Trossard became the second new face in the Brighton squad as new head coach Graham Potter began to shape his group for the 2019/20 campaign. The 24-year-old winger was signed from Belgian side KRC Genk where he inspired the club to the Jupiler Pro League title with 14 goals. He also netted an impressive eight goals from eleven games in Genk's Europa League campaign. An exciting talent, Trossard signed a four-year deal with the Seagulls.

Pascal GROSS

13

POSITION: Midfielder   **COUNTRY:** Germany   **DOB:** 15/06/1991

Following his arrival from FC Ingolstadt ahead of the Seagulls' first Premier League campaign, attacking midfielder Pascal Gross enjoyed an excellent 2017/18 season with Albion. After scoring the all-important goal that ensured Premier League survival, he was voted the club's Player of the Season in 2017/18. One of the first names on the Albion team sheet again in 2018/19, he scored three goals in 25 Premier League outings as Brighton once again secured top-flight status.

SQUAD 2019//20

BRIGHTON &

HOVE ALBION

2019/20

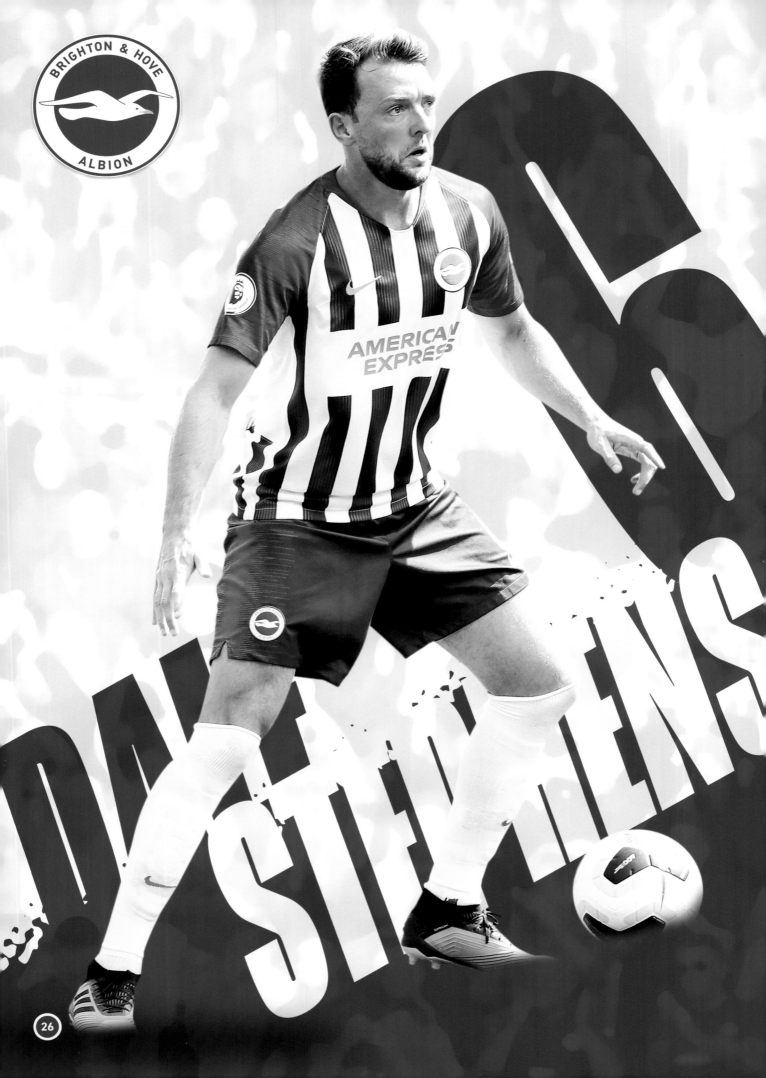

Colour these Brighton stars!

GOAL!

27

Adam
WEBSTER
15

POSITION: Defender **COUNTRY:** England **DOB:** 04/01/1995

A 2019 summer signing from Bristol City, central defender Adam Webster is sure to add both cover and competition at the heart of the Seagulls' defence. His move to Brighton certainly signalled something of a return home for the Chichester-born defender. Webster began his career with Portsmouth before joining Ipswich Town. He moved on from Portman Road to Bristol City in 2018 and his performances for the Robins soon saw him recognised as one of the finest defenders in the Championship.

Leon
BALOGUN
14

POSITION: Defender **COUNTRY:** Nigeria **DOB:** 28/06/1988

Nigerian defender Leon Balogun arrived at Brighton with a wealth of experience in Germany's Bundesliga following spells with FSV Mainz 05, Hannover and Werder Bremen. He made his Premier League debut in Albion's memorable 3-2 victory over Manchester United at the Amex. Balogun appeared in seven further Premier League fixtures and two FA Cup ties in 2018/19. He will be keen to show his worth to new head coach Graham Potter as he seeks further first-team opportunities.

Alireza
JAHANBAKHSH
16

POSITION: Striker **COUNTRY:** Iran **DOB:** 11/08/1993

Alireza Jahanbakhsh became Brighton's record signing when he joined from AZ Alkmaar in July 2018. The Iranian international was the 2017/18 top scorer in Eredivisie, when he scored 21 goals in 33 appearances for AZ. The striker has more than 40 caps for Iran and featured in all three of the country's games at the 2018 FIFA World Cup in Russia. Jahanbakhsh made his Albion debut on the opening day of the 2018/19 season.

Glenn
MURRAY
17

POSITION: Striker   **COUNTRY:** England   **DOB:** 25/09/1983

Ace marksman Glenn Murray has enjoyed two goalscoring spells with Brighton and has twice sampled the joy of securing promotion with the Seagulls. In his initial spell at the club he scored 22 goals in the 2010/11 League One title-winning season. Murray again proved to be the focal point of the attack for Chris Hughton's side in 2016/17 and weighed in with 23 goals as Brighton secured promotion to the Premier League. The experienced frontman has since excelled at Premier League level and is now closing in on Tommy Cook's all-time goalscoring record of 123 goals for Albion.

SQUAD
2019/20

The 2018/19 season saw a number of impressive performances from the Seagulls, here are three to remember...

REWIND

Albion 3
Manchester United 2

A memorable game against the Red Devils saw Albion stun Jose Mourinho's side by scoring three first-half goals. Glenn Murray opened the Seagulls' account on 25 minutes, with a deft flick past David de Gea, and the Amex crowd was still in raptures when Shane Duffy made it two after connecting with a Pascal Gross cut-back.

United halved the deficit in the 34th minute through Romelu Lukaku but the cushion was restored shortly before the break when Gross netted from the penalty spot, having been brought down by Eric Bailly. United also netted from the spot shortly before the end through Paul Pogba, but the margin of victory was bigger than the scoreline suggests.

Crystal Palace 1
Albion 2

The Seagulls completed the double over rivals Crystal Palace for the first time since 1983/84, thanks to Anthony Knockaert's stunning 74th-minute strike.

Glenn Murray opened Albion's account in the first half when he latched on to Lewis Dunk's long ball forward, before steering a superb half-volley past keeper Vicente Guaita. Palace then got back on level terms in the 50th minute through a Luka Milivojevic penalty, before Knockaert took centre stage.

Picking up the ball on the right-hand touchline, the winger cut inside before curling the ball into the top corner that rippled the back of Guaita's net. Cue wild scenes among the travelling support, which were repeated at the final whistle.

Manchester City 1
Albion 0

While it was a game that ended in defeat, the occasion was memorable for Albion fans given it was only the club's second appearance ever in an FA Cup semi-final.

Facing the Premier League champions-elect, the Seagulls got off to the worst possible start when Kevin De Bruyne's teasing right-wing cross was met by Gabriel Jesus, who headed home with just four minutes on the clock.

Other teams would have crumbled given the quality of opposition, but roared on by 34,000 Seagulls fans at Wembley, Albion stood up to City's attacking intent and also created chances of their own.

Indeed, City were grateful to defender Aymeric Laporte's second-half clearance from under his own crossbar with Glenn Murray poised to score, and although City booked their place in the final, Albion received a standing ovation for their effort and endeavour.

Answer these questions on the 2018/19 campaign and see how much attention you were paying LAST SEASON!

1. Who made the most Premier League appearances for the Seagulls last season?

ANSWER

2. Who put in the most Premier League tackles last season?

ANSWER

3. How many points did Brighton finish the 2018/19 season with?

ANSWER

4. How many Premier League goals did the Seagulls score last season?

ANSWER

5. What was the highest home attendance of 2018/19?

ANSWER

6. Against which two clubs did the Seagulls hit three goals last season?

ANSWER

7. Who made the most Premier League passes for Brighton last season?

ANSWER

8. Who knocked Brighton out of the FA Cup in the semi-final?

ANSWER

9. Who received the most yellow cards in the Premier League last season?

ANSWER

10. Who did Brighton sign from Mainz 05 in summer 2018?

ANSWER

11. How many Premier League clean sheets did Brighton keep last season?

ANSWER

12. Who top-scored for the Seagulls last season with 13 Premier League goals?

ANSWER

ANSWERS ON PAGE 62

FAST FORWARD

There are lots of exciting games ahead for the Seagulls in the second half of the 2019/20 Premier League campaign.

Here are three potential crackers...

Chelsea (H)
January 1

Albion kick off 2020 with a mouthwatering home game against Chelsea.

The Blues will have a new man at the helm, Frank Lampard, and without the presence of playmaker Eden Hazard – so often a thorn in Albion's side – or any new signings this season at Stamford Bridge, Graham Potter's men will look to start the New Year with a big three points against the Europa Cup holders. Albion are also looking for their first win against the Blues in the Premier League, having lost all four previous encounters.

Crystal Palace (H)
February 29

The Seagulls will be looking to continue their recent impressive home record against their big rivals from south London. Indeed, Albion are unbeaten against the Eagles in three games at the Amex, with last season's Premier League victory particularly memorable.

While Glenn Murray handed the Seagulls an early lead, Shane Duffy was red carded in the 28th minute, only for his replacement – Leon Balogun – to make an immediate impact, scoring with a superb volley. Florin Andone also netted a fine solo goal before half-time, and although Luka Milivojevic scored a late penalty, ten-man Albion were worthy of all three points. Let's hope history repeats itself!

Manchester United (H)
April 4

As we enter the final weeks of the campaign, Albion face a tough April, with home games against Manchester United, Liverpool and Manchester City. It's therefore important that the Seagulls get the month off to a winning start, with the Red Devils visiting the Amex.

United do not have happy memories of their recent games in Sussex, where they have returned empty-handed from their two Premier League visits. In 2017/18, Pascal Gross scored the only goal which all but secured Albion's top-flight status, so another three points this time will hopefully prove just as important come the end of the season.

PREMIER LEAGUE

OUR PREDICTION FOR PREMIER LEAGUE WINNERS:
MANCHESTER CITY

YOUR PREDICTION:

OUR PREDICTION FOR PREMIER LEAGUE RUNNERS-UP:
LIVERPOOL

YOUR PREDICTION:

CHAMPIONSHIP

OUR PREDICTION FOR CHAMPIONSHIP WINNERS:
DERBY COUNTY

YOUR PREDICTION:

OUR PREDICTION FOR CHAMPIONSHIP RUNNERS-UP:
MIDDLESBROUGH

YOUR PREDICTION:

THE FA CUP

OUR PREDICTION FOR FA CUP WINNERS:
BRIGHTON & HA

YOUR PREDICTION:

OUR PREDICTION FOR FA CUP RUNNERS-UP:
LEICESTER CITY

YOUR PREDICTION:

EFL CUP

OUR PREDICTION FOR EFL CUP WINNERS:
WEST HAM UNITED

YOUR PREDICTION:

OUR PREDICTION FOR EFL CUP RUNNERS-UP:
CHELSEA

YOUR PREDICTION:

2020 PREDICTIONS

TEAMWORK

Every Premier League team is hidden in the grid, except one!
Can you figure out which is missing?

Arsenal

Aston Villa

Bournemouth

Brighton and
Hove Albion

Burnley

Chelsea

Crystal Palace

Everton

Leicester City

Liverpool

Manchester City

Manchester
United

**Newcastle
United**

Norwich City

Sheffield United

Southampton

**Tottenham
Hotspur**

Watford

**West Ham
United**

Wolverhampton
Wanderers

```
J T S E W A K B M R R A T S T C B
E S O T E A S T O N V I L L A R Y
A Q E T S N N B H T E U F T E Y S
E B A O T A P R U V P B K Q O S D
V O J D H E S I M R D B I E V T N
I U T C A W N G E B N U C H I A Z
F R X E M R L H E Y F L K J M L P
M N J G U S I T A I Y O E A E P U
A E H O N R U O N M H X G Y P A S
O M B N I E S N F J H L N W L L A
Y O D K T R Z A N J M O D Q R A P
T U E Z E E H N O H R E T A E C Y
I T T Y D D S D R K L E S S A E T
C H I U F N J H W I S B L S P C I
R N N D A A S O I W U E F P B U C
E F U H G W H V C A H M X D V B R
T E E I F N T E H C N F C G L Y E
S P L R F O E A C D C J I E T V T
E Y T N S T G L I V E R P O O L S
C W S O S P E B T R P G N Y F K E
I W A I V M D I Y V R I B E V H H
E Z C N D A K O E H X E M V I O C
L Q W E L H R N G O M O A E C H N
S M E J K R J S E W R N R R K U A
M A N C H E S T E R U N I T E D M
J A H G U V X B N N I G G O U T H
D I X A F L W M M Y A C L N V H C
C S D O J O L E K Y Z L T B Q S X
K Q B N T W A T F O R D W S Z I P
L F B Y U H N O T P M A H T U O S
```

Q Ex-Hammer who made his debut for the Golden Boys last season

Middlesbrough keeper who played all 46 league games last season **R**

Joint Premier League top scorer last season alongside teammate Mané and Arsenal's Aubameyang **S**

N France international who joined Spurs from Olympique Lyonnais in July 2019

 O

Goalkeeper and local lad who came through the ranks at Norwich

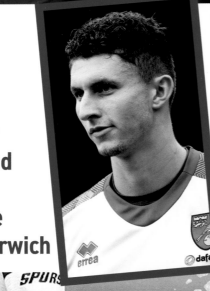

Nickname of Yorkshire club Barnsley **T**

U The Clarets' team kit manufacturer

Former England international in the manager's seat at Craven Cottage **P**

The home of Championship new boys Charlton Athletic **V**

W Managed the Blades to promotion to the Premier League

X Switzerland international who plays his home games at the Emirates Stadium

BRIGHTON & HOVE ALBION

2019/20 PART 2

WHO'S WHO & WHAT'S WHAT OF ENGLISH FOOTBALL?

Y Nottingham Forest's Argentine defensive midfielder

Z Hammers defender capped over 50 times by Argentina

ANSWERS ON PAGE 62

BRIGHTON & HOVE ALBION

Aaron
MOOY
18

POSITION: Midfielder   **COUNTRY:** Australia   **DOB:** 15/09/1990

Australian international midfielder Aaron Mooy joined the Seagulls in the summer of 2019 after agreeing a season-long loan from Huddersfield Town. Mooy was a star performer for the Terriers in their 2016/17 promotion-winning campaign and continued to impress for Huddersfield at Premier League level. With the ability to chip in with goals from midfield, Mooy looks all set to be a popular addition to the Seagulls' squad.

SQUAD 2019/20

José
IZQUIERDO
19

POSITION: Striker **COUNTRY:** Colombia **DOB:** 07/07/1992

José Izquierdo joined Brighton in the summer of 2017 from Club Brugge when he put pen to paper on a four-year contract at the Amex. Izquierdo began his professional career with hometown club Deportivo Pereira. He was a Belgian cup winner with Brugge in 2015 and is also a full Colombian international who played in the 2018 FIFA World Cup finals. He fired his first Premier League goal against West Ham United at the London Stadium in October 2017.

Ezequiel
SCHELOTTO
21

POSITION: Defender **COUNTRY:** Italy **DOB:** 23/05/1989

Vastly experienced full-back Ezequiel Schelotto joined the Seagulls from Sporting Lisbon at the end of the summer transfer window in 2017. A full Italian international, Schelotto names both Parma and Inter Milan among his former clubs. The tough-tackling full-back soon became a popular character among the Albion fans across 20 Premier League outings in his first season at the Amex. He spent a period on loan at Chievo in 2018/19 but injury cut short his time back in Italy.

Solly
MARCH
20

POSITION: Midfielder **COUNTRY:** England **DOB:** 20/07/1994

A tricky wide man who is blessed with natural pace, Solly March enjoyed a highly impressive 2018/19 campaign for the Seagulls. March made 37 appearances in all competitions as Brighton secured their Premier League status while also enjoying a successful FA Cup run. It was March who netted Albion's last-gasp equaliser in the FA Cup quarter-final tie away to Millwall that forced extra time and a memorable penalty shoot-out victory.

BURNLEY
TURF MOOR
CAPACITY: 22,546

MANCHESTER CITY
ETIHAD STADIUM
CAPACITY: 55,097

MANCHESTER UTD
OLD TRAFFORD
CAPACITY: 76,000

EVERTON
GOODISON PARK
CAPACITY: 39,572

LIVERPOOL
ANFIELD
CAPACITY: 54,074

LEICESTER CITY
KING POWER STADIUM
CAPACITY: 32,312

WOLVES
MOLINEUX STADIUM
CAPACITY: 31,700

ASTON VILLA
VILLA PARK
CAPACITY: 42,785

WATFORD
VICARAGE ROAD
CAPACITY: 21,577

SOUTHAMPTON
ST MARY'S STADIUM
CAPACITY: 32,384

BOURNEMOUTH
VITALITY STADIUM
CAPACITY: 11,329

NEWCASTLE UTD
ST JAMES' PARK
CAPACITY: 52,405

PREMIER LEAGUE GROUNDS 2019/20

Get a quick look at where the Seagulls will be heading this season to take on their rivals.

Tick the grounds off once we've visited!

SHEFFIELD UTD
BRAMALL LANE
CAPACITY: 32,702

NORWICH CITY
CARROW ROAD
CAPACITY: 27,244

ARSENAL
EMIRATES STADIUM
CAPACITY: 60,260

TOTTENHAM HOTSPUR
TOTTENHAM HOTSPUR STADIUM
CAPACITY: 62,062

WEST HAM UTD
LONDON STADIUM
CAPACITY: 66,000

CRYSTAL PALACE
SELHURST PARK
CAPACITY: 25,456

CHELSEA
STAMFORD BRIDGE
CAPACITY: 41,631

BRIGHTON & HA
AMERICAN EXPRESS COMMUNITY STADIUM
CAPACITY: 30,666

THE LEGEND GLENN MURRAY

A £300,000 signing from Rochdale during the 2008 January transfer window, Glenn Murray wasted little time in showing the Brighton fans just what he was all about. The striker marked his home debut with a first-half brace as Albion defeated Crewe Alexandra 3-0 in a League One match at Withdean on Saturday, 2 February 2008.

A consistent scorer in an Albion shirt from day one with the Seagulls, Murray netted his first hat-trick for the club in an eventful 3-3 League One draw at home to Cheltenham Town in October 2008. The striker must have known it was going to be his day – his first goal of the afternoon came in the first minute! This hat-trick against the Robins came in a spell of seven goals in four games for the ace marksman.

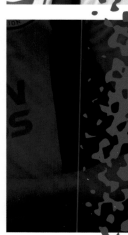

Glenn Murray hammered home an impressive 22 goals in all competitions in the 2010/11 season as Brighton were crowned League One champions. He certainly got the calendar year of 2011 off to a bang by netting a New Year's Day hat-trick in the 5-0 thrashing of Leyton Orient as the Seagulls continued their surge to the Championship.

Now in his second spell with Albion, Murray netted a memorable Amex Stadium hat-trick during the Seagulls' 2016/17 promotion-winning campaign. Norwich City were the visitors and Murray was in scintillating form, he opened the scoring after just six minutes, and then added his second on the hour. He completed his treble after 73 minutes of a 5-0 victory over the Canaries.

Murray was Albion's two-goal hero as the club secured its first Premier League away win in October 2017. In what was Albion's first trip to West Ham's new Olympic Stadium, Murray opened the scoring after ten minutes and then kept his cool to wrap up the three points when he converted a 75th-minute penalty to secure a memorable 3-0 Friday night success in East London.

ANSWERS ON PAGE 62

Martín
MONTOYA

22

POSITION: Defender   **COUNTRY:** Spain   **DOB:** 14/04/1991

Defender Martín Montoya enjoyed an impressive first season in English football having joined Albion from Valencia in August 2018. The former Barcelona and Inter Milan man made his Brighton debut as the Seagulls defeated Manchester United 3-2 at the Amex. He totalled 29 appearances in all competitions as Brighton ensured Premier League survival and also reached the FA Cup semi-final.

SQUAD 2019/20

Jason
STEELE

23

POSITION: Goalkeeper   **COUNTRY:** England   **DOB:** 18/08/1990

Former England Under-21 stopper Jason Steele joined the goalkeeping ranks at the Amex in the summer of 2018 following the end of his contract with Sunderland. An experienced keeper, Steele has amassed over 300 career games following stints at Middlesbrough, Northampton Town, Blackburn Rovers and Sunderland. His Albion debut came in the 3-1 FA Cup third round victory away to Bournemouth.

Davy PRÖPPER 24

POSITION: Midfielder **COUNTRY:** Holland **DOB:** 02/09/1991

Dutch midfielder Davy Pröpper was another player who joined Albion following the club's promotion to the Premier League in 2017. Recruited from PSV Eindhoven, the midfielder soon made a place in the side his own and was a mainstay of the Albion team in his first two seasons with the club. Pröpper clearly impressed new head coach Graham Potter ahead of the 2019/20 campaign as was named in the starting line-up once again for Albion's opening day victory at Watford.

THE LEGEND ANTHONY KNOCKAERT

A first Brighton & Hove Albion goal came Anthony Knockaert's way a month after his arrival from Standard Liege. The Frenchman netted the opening goal in a 3-0 Championship victory over Brentford at the Amex Stadium on 5 February 2016. He ended the season with five goals and his popularity with the Albion fans was well underway.

The main man in the Seagulls' 2016/17 promotion to the Premier League, Knockaert weighed in with 15 goals and none more vital than his brace away to Wolves on 14 April 2017. With the promotion run-in underway and the pressure on to keep delivering results, Knockaert picked the perfect time to show his class. He opened the scoring on the stroke of half-time and netted the second goal in a 2-0 win eight minutes from the end. Victory left the Seagulls on the brink of promotion.

Capping off a truly memorable campaign for the Frenchman, Knockaert was named the EFL's Championship Player of the Season at the end of 2016/17 season. The award was a fitting end to the player's season when he showed outstanding commitment, consistency and exhilarating form – and all against a backdrop of personal tragedy after his father Patrick had sadly died in November 2016.

After starring in Brighton's 2016/17 promotion-winning campaign, Knockaert netted a memorable first Premier League goal when the Seagulls entertained Everton at the Amex on 15 October 2017. A first Premier League goal was a career highlight and the strike gave Albion a 1-0 lead with only eight minutes remaining. Knockaert's effort really should have been enough for all three points but the Toffees took a slight edge off Anthony's day with a last-minute penalty.

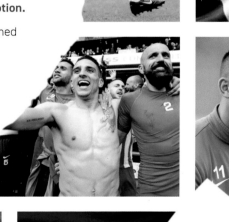

Knockaert wrote his name into Brighton folklore when he struck a stunning winner away to arch-rivals Crystal Palace in March 2019. With the match level at 1-1 and with 16 minutes remaining, the talented Frenchman picked the ball up in front of the travelling Seagulls' fans and hammered home a dramatic winner to spark pandemonium among the Brighton support. The goal sealed a 2-1 win and a Premier League double over the Eagles.

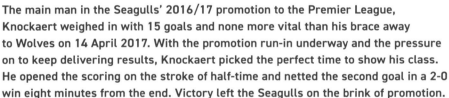

PREMIER
LEAGUE 2019/20

ARSENAL

ASTON VILLA

BOURNEMOUTH

BRIGHTON & HA

BURNLEY

CHELSEA

CRYSTAL PALACE

EVERTON

LEICESTER CITY

In a blue-and-white world, get to know your rivals in full Premier League colour!

LIVERPOOL

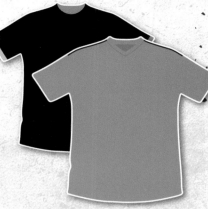

MANCHESTER CITY

MANCHESTER UNITED

NEWCASTLE UNITED

NORWICH CITY

SHEFFIELD UNITED

SOUTHAMPTON

TOTTENHAM HOTSPUR

WATFORD

WEST HAM UNITED

WOLVES

SHANE DUFFY

2018/19

PLAYER OF THE SEASON

Centre-back Duffy fought off some stiff competition, most notably from his defensive partner Lewis Dunk and midfielder Davy Pröpper, to win Albion's coveted Player of the Season award.

The Republic of Ireland international was, again, a model of consistency all season where his commanding presence in the air and his perfectly timed interceptions really caught the eye. Duffy also proved to be an important asset at the other end of the pitch, scoring five times, including the all-important second goal against Manchester United at home.

"I feel as if I'm improving year on year and obviously scoring goals has helped me achieve more recognition," says 'Duffer'. "I was disappointed not to get on the score sheet the previous season, but that changed last season and it was nice to help the team at the other end of the pitch.

"I think I've matured a lot; I'm a year older and I've played a lot of games at this level now. I feel like I've come a long way and have got that consistency to my game."

Duffy also cited his partnership with the Players' Player of the Season, Lewis Dunk, as another reason why his form has gone from strength to strength over the past year.

"We know our roles and our responsibilities going into every game and that helps us. The competition for places at the back has also gone up, with Dan [Burn] and Leon [Balogun] coming into the squad, and that has helped bring both our games on too."

ACADEMY PLAYER
OF THE SEASON

AARON CONNOLLY

The Under-23 striker won the American Express Elite Performance award last season and backed it up by then winning the Premier League 2 Player of the Season award, having ended the season as the league's top scorer with eleven goals.

The Republic of Ireland youngster also ended the campaign on loan at League Two champions Luton Town, having recovered from a hamstring injury which ruled him out for two months.

"It was the best, but also the toughest season I've had with the injury," he reflected. *"Hopefully I can go through a full season without injuries now and break into the first team."*

David BUTTON 27

POSITION: Goalkeeper   COUNTRY: England   DOB: 27/02/1989

A much-travelled and experienced goalkeeper, David Button arrived at the Amex Stadium in the summer of 2018 to provide both competition and cover for the No.1 position. Signing from Fulham having helped the Cottagers win promotion in his final season at Craven Cottage, Button made his Albion debut in the League Cup tie with south coast rivals Southampton. He marked his first Premier League outing for the Seagulls with a clean sheet in the 1-0 home win over Everton in December 2019.

Tudor BĂLUȚĂ 28

POSITION: Midfielder   COUNTRY: Romania   DOB: 27/03/1999

Tudor Băluță joined Albion in January 2019 on a three-and-a-half-year deal from Romanian side FC Viitorul Constanta. The deal saw him return to FC Viitorul on loan for the remainder of the 2018/19 campaign, where he ended the season as part of the side that lifted the Romanian Cup. The 20-year-old has already won international recognition with Romania. After impressing Graham Potter during pre-season, Băluță will look to continue his development throughout the 2019/20 campaign.

SQUAD 2019/20

BERNARDO

30

POSITION: Defender   **COUNTRY:** Brazil   **DOB:** 14/05/1995

Bernardo arrived at Brighton & Hove Albion from RB Leipzig in July 2018. He began his career at Audax São Paulo before moving to Red Bull Brasil in 2012 and then joining Red Bull Salzburg at the start of 2016. Bernardo switched to RB Leipzig in Germany that summer and went on to make 49 appearances for the Bundesliga side. The Brazilian made his Albion debut against Watford in August 2018, and made 27 appearances in his first season at the club.

Dan
BURN

33

POSITION: Defender   **COUNTRY:** England   **DOB:** 09/05/1992

Towering central defender Dan Burn joined the Seagulls in August 2018 from Wigan Athletic. Burn was then loaned back to the Latics for the first half of the 2018/19 season and he featured in 14 Championship fixtures before returning to Brighton at the end of the calendar year. He made his Albion debut in the FA Cup fourth-round match with West Bromwich Albion and also started the replay victory over the Baggies plus the fifth-round triumph over Derby County.

Aaron
CONNOLLY

44

POSITION: Striker   **COUNTRY:** Republic of Ireland   **DOB:** 28/01/2000

Republic of Ireland Under-21 international striker Aaron Connolly moved to Brighton from Irish club Mervue United in 2016. After showing impressive form as a consistent goalscorer for the Academy Under-23 side, his first team debut came against Barnet in the League Cup 2017. He spent the end of 2018/19 on loan with Luton Town and certainly impressed head coach Graham Potter on his return to the Amex. Connolly scored his first goal of the club in the 2019/20 League Cup victory over Bristol Rovers and then got his first taste of Premier League action when he entered the fray against champions Manchester City in August 2019.

Steven
ALZATE

46

POSITION: Striker   **COUNTRY:** England   **DOB:** 08/09/1998

Striker Steven Alzate moved to Brighton & Hove Albion from Leyton Orient in the summer of 2017 after progressing through the youth ranks at Brisbane Road. The Seagulls agreed for him to join League Two Swindon Town on loan for the 2018/19 season but his time at the County Ground was cut short due to injury. He returned to Brighton and after gaining full fitness he made his first team debut in the 2-1 win away to Bristol Rovers in the League Cup in August 2019.

56

The Seagulls have boasted a wealth of talent over the years! Here is our...

SEAGULLS DREAM TEAM

...see if you agree!

GOALKEEPER

MICHEL KUIPERS

Popular Dutch goalkeeper Michel Kuipers experienced an eventful ten-year spell with Brighton after joining the Seagulls in 2000. His career at Withdean saw him play almost 250 league games for the club and enjoy back-to-back promotions in 2000/01 and 2001/02 as the Seagulls soared from the fourth tier to the second.

YOUR CHOICE

RIGHT-BACK

GARY STEVENS

With the ability to operate in either full-back berth or in a central role, Gary Stevens progressed through the youth and reserve ranks at the Goldstone Ground to be a polished top-flight defender. He scored the Seagulls' equalising goal in the 1983 FA Cup Final.

YOUR CHOICE

MIDFIELDER

JIMMY CASE

Jimmy Case proved to be the inspirational driving force behind Brighton's memorable run to the 1983 FA Cup Final at Wembley. He netted vital goals in the matches away to Liverpool, at home to Norwich City and in the semi-final victory over Sheffield Wednesday.

YOUR CHOICE

MIDFIELDER

BRIAN HORTON

Goalscoring midfielder Brian Horton skippered the Seagulls from the Third Division to the First. He was top scorer in the 1978/79 promotion campaign as Brighton reached the top flight. He scored 33 league goals from midfield before joining Luton Town in 1981/82.

YOUR CHOICE

MIDFIELDER

VICENTE

Pacy Spanish winger Vicente joined the Seagulls in September 2011 from Valencia. His outstanding pace and skill swiftly made him a popular player with the Brighton crowd who loved his attacking approach to the game. He further endeared himself to the supporters with a brace against south coast rivals Portsmouth in a 2-0 victory in March 2012.

YOUR CHOICE

LEFT-BACK

BRIDGE
3

WAYNE BRIDGE

England left-back Wayne Bridge produced a series of polished displays for the Seagulls while on loan from Manchester City during the 2012/13 season. Bridge chipped in with three Championship goals as Brighton reached the end-of-season Play-Offs following a fourth-place finish.

YOUR CHOICE

DEFENDER

FOSTER
4

STEVE FOSTER

Central defender Steve Foster joined the Seagulls from south coast rivals Portsmouth in July 1979 following Albion's promotion to the First Division. Twice voted Brighton's Player of the Season, Foster was capped by England during his time at the Goldstone Ground. Suspended for the FA Cup Final in 1983, he captained the team in the replay.

YOUR CHOICE

DEFENDER

LAWRENSON
5

MARK LAWRENSON

Recruited from Preston North End in the summer of 1977, pacy central defender Mark Lawrenson was the Seagulls' Player of the Season in the 1978/79 promotion-winning season as top-flight football finally arrived in Sussex. Lawrenson played 152 league matches for Albion before enjoying a trophy-laden career with Liverpool.

YOUR CHOICE

FORWARD

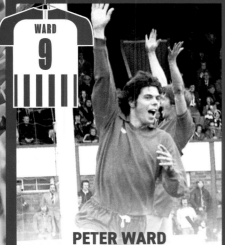

WARD
9

PETER WARD

Striker Peter Ward plundered a club record 32 league goals in the Seagulls' 1976/77 Third Division promotion-winning season. His goals continued to propel Brighton though the divisions as top-flight status was secured in 1979.

YOUR CHOICE

FORWARD

ZAMORA
10

BOBBY ZAMORA

Goalscoring legend Bobby Zamora enjoyed two spells with the club and his £100,000 transfer from Bristol Rovers in 2000 remains one of the club's best value buys. During his first full season he netted an incredible 31 goals as Brighton won the Third Division title in 2000/01.

YOUR CHOICE

MIDFIELDER

KNOCKAERT
11

ANTHONY KNOCKAERT

A star performer in the Seagulls' 2016/17 promotion to the Premier League, Anthony Knockaert ended a memorable campaign as Albion's Player of the Season. He contributed 15 goals from 45 appearances as Brighton sealed the runners-up slot in the Championship.

YOUR CHOICE

TOP 10

MOMENTS OF THIS YEAR

1.
2.
3.
4.
5.
6.
7.
8.
9.
10.

MY TOP 10...

FOOTBALLERS OF ALL TIME

1.
2.
3.
4.
5.
6.
7.
8.
9.
10.

MY TOP 10...

BRIGHTON & HA MEMORIES

1.
2.
3.
4.
5.
6.
7.
8.
9.
10.

MY TOP 10...

RESOLUTIONS FOR 2020

1.
2.
3.
4.
5.
6.
7.
8.
9.
10.

11 TROSSARD

ANSWERS

PAGE 14 · A–Z PART ONE

A. César Azpilicueta. B. Bristol City.
C. Matty Cash. D. Harlee Dean. E. The Eagles.
F. Thomas Frank, Brentford. G. Goodison Park.
H. Neil Harris. I. Kelechi Iheanacho. J. Gabriel Jesus.
K. Mateusz Klich. L. Jesse Lingard. M. Glenn Murray.

PAGE 31 · REWIND

1. Lewis Dunk, 36 appearances. 2. Dale Stephens,
84 tackles. 3. 36. 4. 35. 5. 30,654 vs Wolverhampton
Wanderers (27 October 2018 – Premier League).
6. Manchester United and Crystal Palace.
7. Lewis Dunk, 1,490 passes. 8. Manchester City.
9. Dale Stephens, 6 yellow cards. 10. Leon Balogun.
11. Seven. 12. Glenn Murray.

PAGE 34 · TEAMWORK

Sheffield United.

PAGE 36 · A–Z PART TWO

N. Tanguy Ndombele. O. Aston Oxborough.
P. Scott Parker. Q. Domingos Quina.
R. Darren Randolph. S. Mo Salah.
T. The Tykes. U. Umbro. V. The Valley.
W. Chris Wilder. X. Granit Xhaka.
Y. Claudio Yacob. Z. Pablo Zabaleta.

PAGE 44 · HEY REF

1. Direct free kick. 2. Indirect free kick.
3. Yellow card – Caution. 4. Red card – Sending off.
5. Obstruction. 6. Substitution. 7. Offside/foul.
8. Penalty. 9. Offside location. 10. Play on.